CW00746386

EUROPEAN COUNTRIES TODAY
SPAIN

EUROPEAN COUNTRIES TODAY

TITLES IN THE SERIES

EUROPEAN COUNTRIES TODAY
SPAIN

Dominic J. Ainsley

MASON CREST

Mason Crest
450 Parkway Drive, Suite D
Broomall, Pennsylvania PA 19008
(866) MCP-BOOK (toll free)

Copyright © 2019 by Mason Crest, an imprint of National Highlights, Inc. All rights reserved. No part of this publication may be reproduced or transmitted in any form or by any means, electronic or mechanical, including photocopying, recording, taping, or any information storage and retrieval system, without permission in writing from the publisher.

First printing
9 8 7 6 5 4 3 2 1

ISBN: 978-1-4222-3991-9
Series ISBN: 978-4222-3977-3
ebook ISBN: 978-1-4222-7806-2

Printed in the United States of America

Library of Congress Cataloging-in-Publication Data

Names: Ainsley, Dominic J., author.
Title: Spain / Dominic J. Ainsley.
Description: Broomall, Pennsylvania : Mason Crest, an imprint of National
  Highlights, Inc., 2019. | Series: European countries today | Includes
  index.
Identifiers: LCCN 2018007584 (print) | LCCN 2018018416 (ebook) | ISBN
  9781422278062 (eBook) | ISBN 9781422239919 (hardback)
Subjects: LCSH: Spain--Juvenile literature.
Classification: LCC DP17 (ebook) | LCC DP17 .A615 2019 (print) | DDC 946--dc23 LC record available at
https://lccn.loc.gov/2018007584

Cover images
Main: *The Alhambra, Granada.*
Left: *Spanish produce.*
Center: *La Sagrada Família Cathedral, Barcelona.*
Right: *Pamplona's famous festival "Fiesta de San Fermin," the running of the bulls.*

QR CODES AND LINKS TO THIRD-PARTY CONTENT

You may gain access to certain third-party content ("Third- Party Sites") by scanning and using the QR Codes that appear in this publication (the "QR Codes"). We do not operate or control in any respect any information, products, or services on such Third-Party Sites linked to by us via the QR Codes included in this publication, and we assume no responsibility for any materials you may access using the QR Codes. Your use of the QR Codes may be subject to terms, limitations, or restrictions set forth in the applicable terms of use or otherwise established by the owners of the Third-Party Sites. Our linking to such Third-Party Sites via the QR Codes does not imply an endorsement or sponsorship of such Third-Party Sites or the information, products, or services offered on or through the Third-Party Sites, nor does it imply an endorsement or sponsorship of this publication by the owners of such Third-Party Sites.

CONTENTS

KEY ICONS TO LOOK FOR:

Words to Understand: These words with their easy-to-understand definitions will increase the reader's understanding of the text while building vocabulary skills.

Sidebars: This boxed material within the main text allows readers to build knowledge, gain insights, explore possibilities, and broaden their perspectives by weaving together additional information to provide realistic and holistic perspectives.

Educational Videos: Readers can view videos by scanning our QR codes, providing them with additional content to supplement the text. Examples include news coverage, moments in history, speeches, iconic sports moments, and much more!

Text-Dependent Questions: These questions send the reader back to the text for more careful attention to the evidence presented there.

Research Projects: Readers are pointed toward areas of further inquiry connected to each chapter. Suggestions are provided for projects that encourage deeper research and analysis.

SPAIN AT A GLANCE

MAP OF EUROPE

The Geography of Spain

Location: southwestern Europe, bordering the
  Mediterranean Sea, North Atlantic Ocean,
  Bay of Biscay, and Pyrenees Mountains;
  southwest of France
  Area: approximately twice the size of Oregon
  total: 195,124 square miles
  (505,370 sq. km)
  land: 192,657 square miles
  (498,980 sq. km)
  water: 2,467 square miles (6,390 sq. km)
Borders: Andorra 40 miles (63 km),
  France 401 miles (646 km), Gibraltar 0.7
  miles (1.2 km), Portugal 760 miles (1,224
  km), Morocco (Ceuta) 5 miles (8 km),
  Morocco (Melilla) 6 miles (10.5 km)
Climate: temperate; clear, hot summers in
  interior, more moderate and cloudy along
  coast; cloudy, cold winters in interior, partly
  cloudy and cool along coast
Terrain: large, flat to dissected plateau
  surrounded by rugged hills; Pyrenees
  Mountains in north
  Elevation extremes:
  lowest point: Atlantic Ocean 0 feet (0 m)
  highest point: Signal de Pico de Teide
  (Tenerife) on Canary Islands 12,198 feet
  (3,718 m)
    Natural Hazards: periodic droughts,
  occasional flooding

Source: www.cia.gov 2017

RUSSIA

GEORGIA

ARMENIA

Flag of Spain

Spain is a large European country lying close to northern Africa. The country has varied landscapes with large areas of scrub, forests, and mountains. Spain became united in 1579 when different independent kingdoms merged together; although the colors of the flag date from the twelfth century and were those of the old kingdom of Aragon. Today's flag dates back to 1938 and the time of the civil war. The "excess" of the yellow band is the result of a maritime requirement to make the Spanish flag more visible at sea.

The People of Spain

Population: 48,958,159 (July 2017 est.)
Ethnic Groups: composite of Mediterranean and Nordic types
Age Structure:
   0–14 years: 15.38%
   15–64 years: 66.63%
   65 years and over: 17.99%
Population Growth Rate: 0.78% (2017 est.)
Birth Rate: 9.2 births/1,000 population
Death Rate: 9.1 deaths/1,000 live births
Migration Rate: 7.8 migrants/1,000 population (2017 est.)
Infant Mortality Rate: 3.3 deaths/1,000 live births
Life Expectancy at Birth: 81.8 years
Total Fertility Rate: 1.5 children born/woman
Religions: Roman Catholic 67.8%, atheist 9.1%, other 2.2%, non-believer 18.4%, unspecified 2.5%
Languages: Castilian Spanish 74% (official language nationwide), Catalan 17%, Galician 7%, Basque 2%
Literacy Rate: 98.8%

Source: www.cia.gov 2017

Words to Understand

archipelago: An expanse of water with many scattered islands.

lowland: Low, flat country.

peninsula: A piece of land extending out into a body of water.

BELOW: Toledo is an ancient city set on a hill, above the plains of Castilla-La Mancha, in central Spain. The city is steeped in history and culture and is famous for its medieval architecture. The historic center was designated a World Heritage Site in 1986.

Chapter One
SPAIN'S GEOGRAPHY & LANDSCAPE

The land of Spain lies on an enormous **peninsula** called Iberia. On a map, the Iberian Peninsula looks like a slightly lopsided square with the top bent toward the east and spread wide where it joins the rest of Europe. Florida, on the southeastern tip of the United States, is a large peninsula—but the Iberian Peninsula is nearly four times the size of Florida. Because it's a peninsula, most of Spain's boundaries are water: the Mediterranean Sea on the south and east, all the way from the Straits of Gibraltar to the French border; and the Atlantic Ocean on the northwest and southwest. Spain also shares land boundaries with France and Andorra along the Pyrenees mountain range in the northeast, and with Portugal in the west. The southern tip of Spain's peninsula is Gibraltar, which it ceded to Great Britain in 1713. Out in the Atlantic Ocean, the Canary Islands also belong to Spain, as do the Balearic Islands in the Mediterranean.

Most of the Iberian Peninsula is a high plateau called the Meseta Central. The plateau is rimmed with mountain ranges. A few lines of mountains dissect the plateau, as do some river valleys. Along the coast are narrow plains.

The Mountains of Spain
The Pyrenees form a solid wall between Spain and France. In past centuries, this natural barrier kept the two nations isolated from one another, but today international railroads and highways cross the lower land at the very eastern and western ends of the mountain range. In the middle of the Pyrenees' long backbone, however, passage is difficult from one country to another. In several places, the craggy peaks tower higher than 9,843 feet (3,000 meters). The highest peak in the Pyrenees, Pico de Aneto, is more than 11,155 feet (3,400

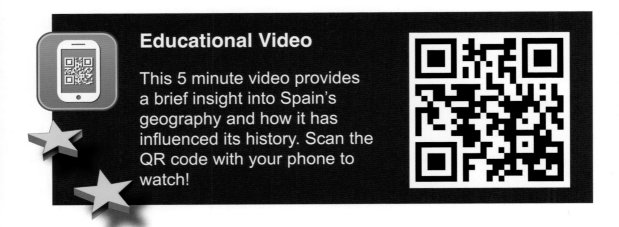

Educational Video

This 5 minute video provides a brief insight into Spain's geography and how it has influenced its history. Scan the QR code with your phone to watch!

meters) high. The highest mountain on the peninsula itself—Mulhacén—is part of the Sierra Nevada that cross Spain south of the city of Granada. The Sierra Nevada Mountains are as high as the Pyrenees: Mulhacén rises to 11,253 feet (3,430 meters), and many other peaks in this range also surpass 9,843 feet (3,000 meters). Other Spanish mountain ranges are the Sierra Morena, the Sistema Ibérico, the Cordillera Cantábrica, and the Sistema Penibético.

ABOVE: *A reservoir high up in the Sierra Nevada Mountains.*

Lowland Regions

Spain's largest lowland region is the Andalusian Plain in the southwest, a wide river valley carved by the Guadalquivir River. As the river nears the Atlantic Ocean, it grows wider until it flows into the Golfo de Cádiz. The Andalusian Plain lies between the Sierra Morena Mountains to the north and the Sistema Penibético to the south. Where these two chains of mountains meet in the east, the plain narrows to an apex.

The Ebro River forms another **lowland** basin, contained by the Sistema Ibérico to the south and west and the Pyrenees to the north and east. A few smaller river valleys are close to the Portuguese border.

ABOVE: *The Guadalquivir River flows from the mountains to the Atlantic Ocean.*

Flora and Fauna

The variety of Spain's landscape is reflected in its flora: among Spain's trees are pines, cork oak trees, and beech trees; its flowering plants include orchids, gentians, lavender, and rosemary.

Spain's native animals are relatively small: deer, ibex, tortoises, bats, snakes (including a venomous viper), and other small creatures; only a small number of bears, wolves, and lynxes remain. Native birds include vultures, eagles, kites, bustards, storks, and flamingos. Many other bird species stop off on their migration routes from Europe to Africa.

ABOVE: *Cantabrian brown bear.*

Along Spain's coasts, between the mountains and the seas, are narrow strips of lowland. They are widest along the Golfo de Cádiz, where the coastal plains join the Andalusian Plain, and along the southern and central eastern coasts. The narrowest coastal plains are along the Bay of Biscay, where the Cordillera Cantábrica Mountains rise up close to the shore.

The Islands

The Balearic Islands are in the Mediterranean, fifty miles (80 kilometers) off Spain's eastern coast. These mountainous islands are actually an extension of the Sistema Penibético that crosses Spain's plateau. The islands form an **archipelago** with a total land area of 193 square miles (500 square kilometers). Their highest point (1,400 feet, or 426 meters) is in Majorca, close to the coast.

ABOVE: *Asturias is a region on the northwest Atlantic coast, located on the Bay of Biscay.*

Spain's other set of islands, the Canaries, which lie fifty-six miles (90 kilometers) off the west coast of Africa, are also mountainous, formed long ago by volcanoes. The highest peaks are in the central islands: Gran Canaria (6,398 feet, or 1,950 meters) and Tenerife (12,139 feet, or 3,700 meters).

ABOVE: *Ibiza is one of the smaller Balearic islands located in the Mediterranean. This rocky island is known for its pine-covered hills and sandy coves. It has lively nightlife in Ibiza Town (above) and also in San Antonio, where large and fashionable nightclubs can be found.*

ABOVE: *The old town of Miravet is on the Ebro River. The Serra de Cardó mountain range is in the background.*

Rivers

Spain has about 1,800 rivers and streams, but most are relatively short; all but ninety are shorter than sixty miles (94 kilometers) long. Only the Tagus is more than 597 miles (960 kilometers) long. For part of each year, the shorter streams are only dry riverbeds. When they do flow, however, they are often fast torrents of water.

Most of Spain's main rivers have their sources in the mountains and flow westward across the plateau into Portugal, eventually emptying into the Atlantic Ocean. The Ebro River, however, flows east, into the Mediterranean. Spain's northwestern coastline is broken by *rías*, narrow inlets between steep rocks, similar to Scandinavia's fjords.

Spain's major rivers include the Duero, the Tejo (or Tagus), the Miño, the Guadiana, and the Guadalquivir. The Guadalquivir is Spain's only navigable inland waterway, making the city of Seville Spain's only inland port for ocean-going ships.

ABOVE: *The town of Nerja is on the Costa del Sol in southern Spain. Nerja enjoys a Mediterranean climate with plenty of sunshine, making it popular with tourists.*

ABOVE: *The Ordesa National Park is in the Pyrenees mountain range. The park is located along the border with France.*

Climate

Spain's main peninsula experiences three climates: continental, maritime, and Mediterranean.

Across most of Spain's central plateau, as well as in the adjoining mountains to the east and south, the temperatures vary greatly between the winter and summer seasons. This land gets little rain, and what rain does fall (usually only 12 to 25 inches, or 30 to 64 centimeters a year) tends to evaporate, leaving the land arid.

The northern region and the Ebro Basin have two rainy seasons, one in spring (from April to June) and the other in fall (October to November). The

ABOVE: *Gaztelugatxe is a small island on the coast of Biscay, near Bermeo, in the Basque country. It is connected to the mainland by a stone bridge. On the island stands the hermitage of San Juan de Gaztelugatxe, which is dedicated to John the Baptist. The hermitage dates from the tenth century.*

Protecting the Environment

Like all countries, Spain has environmental problems, including deforestation, soil erosion, and sea pollution. The huge success of the tourist industry has brought more pollution to Spain. Five national parks and hundreds of protected areas and reserves, however, have been established over the years.

southern portion of the Meseta also has spring and fall rainy seasons, but the spring one is earlier (March). In the north, the spring is the wetter time of the year, while in the south the fall is wetter. Even during these rainy seasons, however, the rain falls unpredictably, and only once in a while.

The winters are cold and windy, while the summers are warm and cloudless. In most of the Meseta, daytime summer temperatures range between 68 degrees and 80 degrees F (20 and 27 degrees C). But the Ebro Basin is very hot during the summer: temperatures can reach higher than 109 degrees F (43 degrees C).

The Maritime Climate

In northern Spain, from the Pyrenees to the northwest region, the sea moderates the weather. The winters are mild and the summers are pleasantly warm without being hot. Abundant rain falls all year round, and the temperatures rise and fall very little. Fall (October through December) is the wettest season, while July is the driest month. Fog and mist are common along the northeast coast.

The Mediterranean Climate

This climatic region runs along the seaward side of the mountain ranges that run parallel to the coast, reaching from the Andalusian Plain along the southern

ABOVE: *Hoya de Guadix is northeast of the city of Granada in Andalusia. Warm winds from North Africa ensure that southern Spain is hot and dry in summer.*

and eastern coasts, up to the Pyrenees. The total annual rainfall in this region is lower than anywhere else in Spain, both in the winter and the summer, with low humidity. January temperatures average 50 to 55 degrees F (10 to 13 degrees C), while in August the temperatures average 72 to 88 degrees F (22 to 31 degrees C).

Winds from North Africa blow over the Mediterranean region. Referred to as the Leveche winds, these hot, dry air currents sometimes carry fine dust from Africa. A cooler wind from the east, the Levante, funnels between the Sistema Penibético Mountains and North Africa's Atlas Mountains.

Spain's geography and climate have helped shape the nation as it is today. They also played a role in this nation's ancient history.

Text-Dependent Questions

1. How many different languages are spoken in Spain?

2. What mountain range divides Spain from France?

3. What are Spain's most important rivers?

Research Project

Draw a map of Spain and mark where the major rivers and mountain ranges are situated.

Words to Understand

Carthaginians: Inhabitants of the ancient city-state of Carthage, which is located in modern-day Tunisia.

Phoenicians: Members of an ancient Semitic people of Syria who dominated the trade of the ancient world.

Visigoths: Members of the western Goths who invaded the Roman Empire in the fourth century and settled in France and Spain.

BELOW: The hill fort of Monte de Santa Tecla is in Galicia. It was discovered in 1913 when excavations were made for a new road. It consists of circular, oval, and square buildings. The later ones show Roman influence.

Chapter Two
THE GOVERNMENT & HISTORY OF SPAIN

Archeologists have found evidence that humans have lived on the Iberian Peninsula for thousands of years. Evidence of Neanderthals has been found in the peninsula dating back to around 200,000 BCE and modern humans arrived on the scene somewhere between 50,000 and 30,000 BCE when they moved in from the east. **Phoenicians** sailed in from the east, creating trading posts along Andalusia's seaboard. Later, around 800 BCE, the Celts (the same people who settled Ireland and Scotland) arrived in the northern third of the

ABOVE: Sagunto Castle is a vast ruin overlooking the town of Sagunto, near Valencia. The site's history extends back over two thousand years and includes Iberian, Roman, and medieval remains. In particular, the site houses the remains of a Roman forum.

Educational Video

The history of the Spanish language.

ABOVE: *The ancient town of Córdoba, Andalusia. The Roman bridge crossing the Guadalquivir River is in the foreground and the Great Mosque is in the background.*

peninsula. By 500 BCE, the **Carthaginians** from northern Africa had colonized what is now southern Spain.

Spain and the Roman Empire

In 206 BCE, the Roman Empire invaded Spain. The Roman soldiers easily crushed the native resistance and soon transformed the Iberian Peninsula into one of Rome's richest and most organized colonies. The Romans built paved roads that criss-crossed the peninsula, and they sailed their galleys up the Guadalquivir, all the way to Córdoba, where they loaded olive oil and wine into their holds for exportation to Rome.

When the Roman Empire adopted Christianity in the fourth century CE, Spain also became a Christian land. The Roman influence was strong on Spanish culture, and today's modern Spanish language still holds strong echoes of Rome's Latin.

Dating Systems and Their Meaning

You might be accustomed to seeing dates expressed with the abbreviations BC or AD, as in the year 1000 BC or the year AD 1900. For centuries, this dating system has been the most common in the Western world. However, since BC and AD are based on Christianity (BC stands for Before Christ and AD stands for anno Domini, Latin for "in the year of our Lord"), many people now prefer to use abbreviations that people from all religions can be comfortable using. The abbreviations BCE (meaning Before Common Era) and CE (meaning Common Era), mark time in the same way (for example, 1000 BC is the same year as 1000 BCE, and AD 1900 is the same year as 1900 CE), but BCE and CE do not have the same religious overtones as BC and AD.

The Visigoths and the Moors

When the Roman Empire collapsed in the fifth century, waves of barbarian tribes swept across Europe. The **Visigoths**, a warlike Germanic people who migrated from central Europe, eventually took control of the Iberian Peninsula.

Their rule was chaotic and disorganized, however, and eventually, in 711, the Moors swept in from Northern Africa. These Muslim people ruled the Iberian Peninsula for more than seven centuries. Yet as Europe's Christian nations grew in power, they gradually drove the Moors further and further south. The last Moorish kingdom, Granada (the eastern half of modern-day Andalusia), fell in 1492 to the Catholic Monarchs, Isabella and Ferdinand. The Moors' cultural legacy can still be seen in Spain, especially in monuments such as the Mosque of Córdoba and the Alhambra Palace in Granada.

ABOVE: *Isabella I of Castile.*

Spain and the New World

Spain played an important role in the discovery of new land on the other side of the Atlantic, since King Ferdinand and Queen Isabella were the sponsors of Christopher Columbus's voyage of exploration. Columbus was followed by the conquistadors, who brought great wealth from the New World to Spain. As the conquistadors conquered more and more of

ABOVE: *Ferdinand II of Aragon by Michel Sittow.*

ABOVE: *Posthumous portrait of Christopher Columbus by Sebastiano del Piombo, 1519.*

the Americas' native peoples, Spain built a vast overseas empire. Spain became one of the strongest and most important nations in the world.

Much of the wealth that Spain gained from the Americas was spent on wars with northern Europe and with the Ottoman Turks in the Mediterranean region. Gradually, the flow of riches from the New World diminished—and so did Spain's power.

ABOVE: The Second of May 1808: The Charge of the Mamelukes *by Francisco de Goya, 1814. The painting is set in the Calle de Alcalá near Puerta del Sol, Madrid, during the Dos de Mayo Uprising. It depicts one of many riots against the French occupation of Spain.*

A Decline in Fortunes

During much of the eighteenth and nineteenth centuries, the nations of Europe were at war with one another. At the beginning of this period, when the Bourbon dynasty took the Spanish throne, Spain came under France's influence for nearly a hundred years. Meanwhile, Spain's South American colonies were demanding independence.

In the nineteenth century, when Napoleon Bonaparte's army was defeated during the Peninsular War, Spain regained its independence. The years that followed, however, were filled with unrest. The Spanish people were divided into opposing groups: the country and city people, the conservatives and the liberals. Violent overthrows of the government happened frequently, but none of the new governments lasted very long.

In the Spanish-American War at the end of the nineteenth century, Spain lost the last of its colonies—Cuba and the Philippines—a loss that proved devastating to Spain's economy and politics. The resulting unrest led to a stronger working class, who, in 1931, forced King Alfonso XIII to abdicate his throne. Spain was declared a republic—but not everyone was happy about this development. Conservative reaction from both the army and the Catholic Church led to the outbreak of the Spanish Civil War. At the end of the war, General Francisco Franco and his nationalist movement took control of the country.

During World War II, Spain did not openly side with either the Allies or the Axis. Unofficially, however, Franco supported the Axis. As a result, after the war, an international blockade was

ABOVE: General Francisco Franco photographed in May 1968.

31

imposed on the country. Spain was ostracized by the community of nations, and the Spanish economy sank even lower. Poverty became all too common across the peninsula.

The Return of Good Fortune

During the Cold War, Spain became strategically attractive to the United States. In the 1950s, American army bases were built in Spain, and tourists eventually came to Spain along with the military personnel. As foreign money began to flow into the country, a large middle class emerged, and the nation's desperate poverty diminished.

When Franco died in 1975, the transition to democracy went fairly smoothly. A democratic constitution was put in effect in 1978, under the symbolic monarchy of King Juan Carlos II. The young monarch resolutely prodded his nation toward Western-style democracy and political reform. Spain's number-one diplomatic goal was to be recognized as a democratic, West European society.

When Franco was in power, the European Community had refused to allow Spain to become a member, but now Prime Minister Adolfo Suárez González sent his foreign minister to Brussels to once more ask that Spain be allowed to join. Negotiations for Spain's entry into the European Community were long and complicated. Even after Spain had made many democratic changes to its government, European Community members still worried about how Spain's economy would affect the European Community. Spain's economy was much less developed than that of other member nations, and its industries needed major reforms. Spanish agriculture was also less developed than in the rest of Europe.

ABOVE: *Prime Minster Adolfo Suárez González.*

Local Governments

Spain's 1978 constitution created regional governments, similar to states or provinces in the United States and Canada. Today, there are seventeen regions. The central federal government is giving the regional governments more and more responsibility. Eventually, they will have full responsibility for health care, education, and other social programs.

After lengthy bargaining, however, these issues were eventually resolved. The Treaty of Accession was signed in the summer of 1985, and on January 1, 1986, Spain finally entered the European Community. The terms of the treaty committed Spain to making major ongoing contributions to the European Community budget, but most Spaniards didn't seem to care. They had finally achieved a long-awaited goal, and now they savored being included in the West European society of nations. As the years went by, polls indicated that most Spaniards had a sense of being "citizens of Europe."

The Parliamentary Monarchy

Today, the Spanish constitution provides for a parliamentary monarchy. The king is a traditional hereditary monarch who acts as head of state and supreme head of the armed forces—but he is not sovereign. Instead, sovereign power is held by a two-chamber parliament, called the Cortes, whose members are elected by the citizens.

The Cortes is made up of the Congress of Deputies and the Senate. The Congress of Deputies is the stronger of the two bodies; it consists of three hundred to four hundred members, elected by proportional representation every four years (unless the king chooses to call for new elections sooner). The

ABOVE: *The Palacio del Senado in Madrid is the headquarters of the Spanish Senate.*

Senate is composed of 208 elected members and 57 regional representatives, who are also elected every four years. Its primary function is territorial representation.

Either house may set a law in motion, but the Congress of Deputies can override a Senate veto. This means that if a political party has a solid majority in the Congress of Deputies, they have enormous political clout. The Congress of Deputies also has the power to officially approve or reject legislation, and it acts as a check against the prime minister's power, since the Congress can vote the prime minister out of office. Each chamber of the Cortes meets in separate buildings in Madrid during two regular annual sessions from September to December and from February to June.

The members of the Spanish parliament enjoy certain special privileges: they may not be prosecuted for verbal opinions expressed in the course of their duties; they cannot be arrested for a crime unless they are caught in the actual act of committing it (and even then, the Cortes must give its consent for them to

ABOVE: *The Congress of Deputies building in Madrid.*

be charged or prosecuted); they are guaranteed a fixed salary and allowances for extra expenses; and they are not obliged to follow their parties' dictates when they cast their votes.

Meanwhile, the king formally convenes and dissolves the Cortes; he also calls for elections and for referendums. He appoints the prime minister after consultation with the Cortes, and he names the other ministers on the recommendation of the prime minister.

Although the king does not have the power to direct foreign affairs, he has a vital role as the chief representative of Spain in international relations. The potential significance of this role has been demonstrated during the reign of Felipe VI, whose many trips abroad and contacts with foreign leaders have enabled the Spanish government to establish important political and commercial ties with other nations. The king also has the duty to indicate the state's consent to international treaties and, with the prior authorization of the Cortes, to declare war and peace.

While the king has a largely symbolic role, the prime minister is the actual leader of the government. The king has the title of supreme commander of the armed forces, but the military is actually under the prime minister's control. Once appointed, the prime minister remains in office until he either resigns, loses the support of the Congress of Deputies, or his party is defeated in the general elections.

The prime minister, the deputy prime minister, and the other government ministers make up the Council of Ministers, which is Spain's highest executive institution. The Council of Ministers is responsible for putting into effect government policy. It is also responsible for national security and defense. In all its functions, however, it is ultimately responsible to the Cortes. The constitution provides that none of the ministers may engage in professional or commercial activity, or hold any additional public posts. During Franco's reign, senior government officials were often leaders of the business community, which led to corruption.

Today's Spain seeks to avoid the mistakes of the past by maintaining a system of government built carefully on compromise between monarchy and democracy, with a well-structured system of checks and balances.

ABOVE: *King Felipe VI and Queen Letizia of Spain on a state visit to Berlin in 2014.*

ABOVE: *The prime minister of Spain Mariano Rajoy, at the European G20 preparatory meeting in Germany in 2017.*

In the elections of March 1996, the Popular Party (PP) came into power and José María Aznar became prime minister of the country. He carried out many changes in the government, and, during his first term of office, Spain joined the eurozone (the region using the euro as currency). After the terrorist attacks on the United States on September 11, 2001, Aznar allied with the Bush administration in the military actions in Iraq. Under Aznar's leadership, Spain also backed the military action against the Taliban in Afghanistan and took a leadership role within the European Union in pushing for increased international cooperation against terrorism.

In 2004, just three days after the terrorist attack on a Madrid commuter train, Aznar's party was voted out of office, and José Luis Rodríguez Zapatero was elected prime minister. Carrying out his campaign promises, Zapatero immediately withdrew Spanish forces from Iraq, but he continued to support Iraq reconstruction efforts and cooperated with the United States on counterterrorism issues. Zapatero was reelected for a second term as prime minister on March 9, 2008, but he announced in April 2011 that he would not run for reelection in 2012. Mariano Rajoy became Spain's next prime minster in 2012 and was reelected for another term on October 29, 2016.

Text-Dependent Questions

1. What did the conquistidors do?

2. What political movement did General Francisco Franco control?

3. When did Mariano Rajoy become prime minister?

Research Project

Write a short biography on General Francisco Franco, who ruled Spain as a military dictator.

The Formation of the European Union (EU)

The EU is a confederation of European nations that continues to grow. As of 2017, there are twenty-eight official members. Several other candidates are also waiting for approval. All countries that enter the EU agree to follow common laws about foreign security policies. They also agree to cooperate on legal matters that go on within the EU. The European Council meets to discuss all international matters and make decisions about them. Each country's own concerns and interests are important, though. And apart from legal and financial issues, the EU tries to uphold values such as peace, human dignity, freedom, and equality.

All member countries remain autonomous. This means that they generally keep their own laws and regulations. The idea for a union among European nations was first mentioned after World War II. The war had devastated much of Europe, both physically and financially. In 1950, the French foreign minister suggested that France and West Germany combine their coal and steel industries under one authority. Both countries would have control over the

ABOVE: The entrance to the European Union Parliament Building in Brussels.

MEMBER COUNTRIES

Austria	Greece	Romania
Belgium	Hungary	Slovakia
Bulgaria	Ireland	Slovenia
Croatia	Italy	Spain
Cyprus	Latvia	Sweden
Czech Republic	Lithuania	United Kingdom
Denmark	Luxembourg	*(Brexit: For the time*
Estonia	Malta	*being, the United*
Finland	Netherlands	*Kingdom remains a full*
France	Poland	*member of the EU.)*
Germany	Portugal	

industries. This would help them become more financially stable. It would also make war between the countries much more difficult. The idea was interesting to other European countries as well. In 1951, France, West Germany, Belgium, Luxembourg, the Netherlands, and Italy signed the Treaty of Paris, creating the European Coal and Steel Community. These six countries would become the core of the EU.

In 1957, these same countries signed the Treaties of Rome, creating the European Economic Community. In 1965, the Merger Treaty formed the European Community. Finally, in 1992, the Maastricht Treaty was signed. This treaty defined the European Union. It gave a framework for expanding the EU's political role, particularly in the area of foreign and security policy. It would also replace national currencies with the euro. The next year, the treaty went into effect. At that time, the member countries included the original six plus another six who had joined during the 1970s and '80s.

In the following years, the EU would take more steps to form a single market for its members. This would make joining the union even more advantageous. In addition to enlargement, the EU is steadily becoming more integrated through its own policies for closer cooperation between member states.

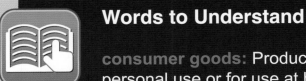

Words to Understand

consumer goods: Products that people buy for personal use or for use at home.

Industrial Revolution: A rapid major change in an economy marked by the general introduction of power-driven machinery.

national debt: The total amount of money that the government of a country owes.

BELOW: There are many holiday resorts in Spain. Benidorm, photographed here, is an important one. Over the years, resorts such as Benidorm, have been vital to the Spanish economy.

Chapter Three
THE SPANISH ECONOMY

During the nineteenth century, when the **Industrial Revolution** was transforming the economies of most western European nations, Spain "missed the boat." Instead, while other nations were turning into modern, mechanized socities, Spain was deep in social and political turmoil.

At the beginning of the twentieth century, most Spaniards lived in the country, dependent on farming. The country had few factories, and even its farms were not as productive as other West European countries'. Spain lacked technology,

ABOVE: *A traditional small Galician farm in Camino de Santiago.*

ABOVE: *San Vicente de la Sonsierra is a town in the wine-growing Rioja region of Spain.*

The Economy of Spain

Gross Domestic Product (GDP): US$1.686 trillion (2016 est.)

GDP per capita: US$36,300 (2016 est.)

Industries: textiles and apparel (including footwear), food and beverages, metals and metal manufactures, chemicals, shipbuilding, automobiles, machine tools, tourism, clay and refractory products, footwear, pharmaceuticals, medical equipment

Agriculture: grain, vegetables, olives, wine grapes, sugar beet, citrus; beef, pork, poultry, dairy products; fish

Export Commodities: machinery, motor vehicles; foodstuffs, pharmaceuticals, medicines, other consumer goods

Export Partners: France 15.2%, Germany 11.4%, Italy 7.8%, UK 7.6%, Portugal 7%, US 4.4% (2016)

Import Commodities: machinery and equipment, fuels, chemicals, semi-finished goods, foodstuffs, consumer goods, measuring and medical control instruments

Import Partners: Germany 14.7%, France 12%, China 7.1%, Italy 6.7%, Netherlands 5.2%, UK 4.4%

Currency: euro

Source: www.cia.gov 2017

its financial institutions were underdeveloped, and the government failed to build the economy. The Spanish Civil War wreaked further havoc on the nation's economy, and Franco did very little to help matters once he came into power.

Not until the 1950s did Spain's economy begin to grow. A second period of economic expansion began in the mid-1980s when Spain entered the European Community (EC, the forerunner of the European Union. The EC required that Spain modernize its industries, improve its infrastructure, and revise its economic laws to conform to EC guidelines. By doing so, Spain was able to reduce its **national debt**, its unemployment rate from 23 percent to 15 percent in just three years, and inflation to less than 3 percent.

By the early twenty-first century, Spain had been transformed from a rural, backward nation of farmers into a country with a diverse economy built on manufacturing and service businesses. However, largely due to the financial crisis of 2007, Spain's budget deficit peaked at 11.4 percent of GDP in 2010, but gradually reduced to about 5 percent of GDP in 2015, and 4.1 percent of GDP in 2016. Unfortunately, though, public debt has increased substantially—from 60.1 percent of GDP in 2010 to nearly 99.5 percent in 2016.

ABOVE: *Catalonians calling for independence from Spain in 2017.*

Educational Video

Catalonia's independence referendum explained.

ABOVE: *The commercial and industrial port of Barcelona, Catalonia.*

Exports and Imports

Spain's most important trading partners are France, Germany, and Italy. Its chief exports are machinery, including motor vehicles, and food products. The country is the world's largest producer of olive oil, the fourth largest of dried fruit, and the sixth largest of citrus fruits. Spain's vineyards are the largest in the world, although it's only the fifth-highest producer of wine-grapes and ranks third in wine production. Its other important crops include barley, wheat, maize, rice, potatoes, sugar beet, peppers, avocados, tomatoes, tobacco, hops, oil-bearing fruits, and cork. Meanwhile, Spain imports machinery and equipment, fuels, chemicals, food, and **consumer goods**.

ABOVE: *The grape harvest. Spain's grape-growing industry is very important for its economy, producing grapes for the table and for the wine-making industry.*

ABOVE: *The El Corte Inglés department store in Barcelona. The store is part of a large group and has its headquarters in Madrid. It is the biggest department store group in Europe.*

Industries

Just five of Spain's provinces (Barcelona, Biscay, Madrid, Navarre, and Oviedo, all located in the north and east) produce over half the country's manufacturing output. The Catalonia region, where some 85 percent of companies are located in Barcelona, is Spain's economic powerhouse and one of Europe's most important industrial regions.

Spanish industry is rooted in small- and medium-sized family businesses; just a few Spanish businesses are known internationally (Telefónica, Endesa, Repsol, and others). Most Spanish manufacturers are too small to compete

ABOVE: Holiday homes are a familiar sight in the coastal areas of Spain. Most homes are sold to foreigners, particulary to the British. This development is near Málaga.

globally. As a result, Spain has relied heavily on foreign investment (three-quarters of it in Barcelona and Madrid) for much of its recent growth.
The Spanish economy is hindered by its lack of modern machinery and technology; many Spanish industrial plants are out of date, with machinery that needs replacing. Spain has had particular difficulty developing computer technology, which puts the nation's industries at a definite disadvantage. Poor efficiency and lack of good business organization further weaken Spanish industries.

Spain's most important industries include tourism, chemicals and petrochemicals, heavy industry, and food and beverages. Its principal growth areas include tourism, insurance, and electronics. Tourism is one of Spain's most important industries, especially in Andalusia.

Once the richest nation in Europe, over the past few centuries Spain has endured poverty and economic recessions. Spain's economy paid the price for the country's isolation from the rest of the world through much of the nineteenth and twentieth centuries.

Then, with the coming of democracy, the Spanish economy was regarded as one of the strongest within the EU. However, the economy depended on its tourism industry, housing market, and construction industry; the global economic crisis of 2008 through 2009 hit the country hard, because fewer people could afford to travel and buy and build new homes. Spain's economy plunged into recession and unemployment became double the EU average. As a result, the goverent introduced austerity to reduce the nation's debt. Spain's recession lasted until 2013. Since then, it has made a steady recovery. Borrowing costs have been reduced and inflation is down, reaching a negative of 0.3 percent in 2016.

Text-Dependent Questions

1. Who are Spain's most important trading partners?

2. Where is Spain's economic powerhouse?

3. When did Spain recover from its last recession?

Research Project

Write a report on what happens to a country's economy it goes into an economic recession.

Words to Understand

federation: A union of organizations or states.

genre: A particular type or category of literature or art.

Iberian: Relating to Spain or Portugal.

BELOW: Bilbao is a city in northern Spain. It is the largest city in the province of Biscay. It is home to great architectural projects that have been the driving force of the urban and economic regeneration of the city.

Chapter Four
CITIZENS OF SPAIN:
PEOPLE, CUSTOMS & CULTURE

For centuries, Spain's people lacked any true unified identity. Its regions, with their varied climates and geography, joined in a loose **federation**, but not until modern times did Spaniards begin to identify themselves with their nation rather than their particular region. Even today, Spain's regions have their own cultural, economic, and political characteristics—and people still feel that their primary loyalty lies with their town or region, and only secondarily with Spain as a whole.

Spain's Population Groups

Around the edges of the **Iberian** Peninsula are groups of people who have competed for centuries for control of the peninsula. The Portuguese to the west are the only group that successfully established its own state (in 1640). The Galicians live along the northwest, and the Asturians are on the northern coast of the Bay of Biscay. The Basques live near the coast toward France, the Navarrese and the Aragonese are along the Pyrenees backbone, the Catalans are in the northeast, the Valencians in the east and in the south are the Andalusians.

Rich Spain and Poor Spain

Economic differences divide Spaniards even more than the cultural differences between the various regions. For the past century, the government has tried to redistribute the country's wealth more fairly, but these differences continue to exist.

If you drew an imaginary line from the middle of the north coast southeast to Madrid and then to Valencia, you could mark the invisible boundary that has existed between "Rich Spain" and "Poor Spain." To the north and east of the line lived the wealthy Spaniards in an area that was modern, industrial, and

ABOVE: *Santiago de Compostela is the capital of northwest Spain's Galicia region. It is situated at the end of the Camino de Santiago pilgrimage route which originated in the nineth century. It is said to be the burial site of the Biblical apostle St. James. His remains reputedly lie within the Cathedral of Santiago de Compostela, consecrated in 1211. In 1985 the city's old town was designated a World Heritage Site.*

urban. By the 1980s, this region was already transitioning to a thriving information and services economy. But to the south and west of that imaginary line lies "Poor Spain," where most people supported themselves by farming. Social conditions here were much different from what they were on the rich side. The separation between the two groups grew even wider when the people of Rich Spain tended to think of themselves as culturally "not-Spanish."

Religion

Despite their differences, Spaniards have one big thing in common: almost all of them (about 94 percent) are Roman Catholic. Back in the fifteenth century, when Ferdinand and Isabella conquered Muslim Spain, they established

Who Are the Basques?

The original name for the Basques (and the one that Basques still use for themselves) is "Euskaldunak." They are a very ancient and unique people who live in northern Spain and southwestern France. Their language is not related to any other language ever seen or recorded, and archeologists believe they have lived in the same region of Europe for thousands of years.

The ETA (Euskadi Ta Askatasuna—meaning "Basque homeland and liberty") began in the 1960s as a student resistance movement against Franco, who was then the dictator of Spain. Under Franco, the Basque language was banned, their culture was suppressed, and many Basques were imprisoned and tortured for their political and cultural beliefs.

The Basques fought hard for freedom from Franco. When he died in 1975, the Basque region gained many rights. The Basques now have their own parliament and police force. Their government controls the education of their children, and it collects its own taxes. But the ETA and its supporters remained determined that the Basques needed full independence and freedom from the rest of Spain. After years of fighting without success, the ETA announced a ceasefire in 2010, followed by an end to armed conflict in 2011. In 2017, ETA revealed the location of weapons caches to police in France and said it had now completely disarmed.

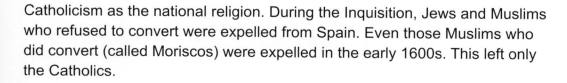

Catholicism as the national religion. During the Inquisition, Jews and Muslims who refused to convert were expelled from Spain. Even those Muslims who did convert (called Moriscos) were expelled in the early 1600s. This left only the Catholics.

Today, however, few Spanish Catholics take their religion quite as seriously as Ferdinand and Isabella did. Catholic ceremonies and festivals are still vital to the flavor of Spanish culture. Though most people get married in a church, and they baptize their children, few Spaniards attend church regularly these days. They look to Catholic traditions to give their lives depth and meaning but tend to not seek practical direction from the Church's teachings.

Spanish Arts and Culture

Architecture Spain is famous for its architecture, particularly its Gothic churches and medieval castles. Even the smallest towns have their own

ABOVE: *Antoni Gaudí's masterpiece, the Casa Milà, is popularly known as La Pedrera. It boasts an impressive central atrium and an incredible roof terrace that commands views of the city of Barcelona. Gaudí avoided straight lines in his buildings, and so they have an organic feel about them. In 1984, the Casa Milà was declared a World Heritage Site.*

Guernica

One of Pablo Picasso's most famous works is *Guernica* (1937), a massive painting commissioned by the Spanish government that depicts the bombing of the Basque city of Guernica. Picasso's canvas is a vivid and brutal portrayal of people, animals, and buildings wrenched by the violent bombing. The painting has become a larger symbol for the entire world, for it embodies the inhumanity and hopelessness of war.

distinctive architectural atmosphere. Every town and village has a *plaza mayor*—main square—often reached by an arcade. The square is usually an extended open courtyard of the town or village hall. From prehistoric monuments in the Balearic Islands to Roman ruins and fantastic modernist constructions, Spain's architecture is some of the most impressive in the world.

Visual Arts Ever since the tenth century, Spain has produced great painters. Two of the most famous are Velázquez (1599–1660) and Goya (1746–1828), who played a significant role in the evolution of painting in Europe. Works by these artists and many others can be seen at the Prado art museum in Madrid. In the twentieth century, Spain's Paris School produced such internationally known names as Salvador Dalí and Pablo Picasso.

The country is also famous for its talented craftsmen. They create carved furniture (particularly chests); tapestries and embroideries; gold, silver, and ironwork (including wrought-iron screens); sculpture; and ceramics.

Music Spain has a rich musical heritage. The guitar was invented in Andalusia in the 1790s, when a sixth string was added to the Moorish lute. By the 1870s, the guitar had gained its modern shape. Spanish musicians have taken the

ABOVE: The Triumph of Baccus, *popularly knowns as* The Drunks *by Diego Velázquez.*

guitar to heights of virtuosity and none more so than Andrés Segovia (1893–1997), who established classical guitar as a musical **genre**.
Guitars are essential to flamenco, Spain's best-known musical tradition. Flamenco has its roots in the *cante jondo* (deep song) of the Roma of Andalusia, but today it is experiencing a revival. Paco de Lucía is an internationally known flamenco guitarist, and Pablo Casals is an equally gifted cellist.

Modern composers such as Enrique Granados, Isaac Albéniz, Manuel de Falla, and Joaquín Rodrigo have also gained international recognition. Plácido Domingo is one of Spain's most famous operatic performers, closely followed by Montserrat Caballé. Originally from Catalonia, Caballé is known to be one of the most outstanding sopranos in the world.

Literature Spain's most famous author is Miguel Cervantes, who wrote *Don Quixote de la Mancha*. This seventeenth-century book is one of the earliest novels written in a modern European language, and many people consider it still to be the finest work ever written in the Spanish language.

The book tells the story of Don Quixote and his squire, Sancho Panza. Don Quixote is obsessed with stories of knights, and his friends and family think he's crazy when he sets out to wander across Spain on Rocinante, his skinny horse, righting wrongs and protecting the oppressed.

Don Quixote sees reality with the eyes of a romantic. He believes ordinary inns are enchanted castles, and peasant girls are beautiful princesses. His head-in-the-clouds dreaminess has become a part of the entire world's imagination. Even in the English language, the word "quixotic," from Don Quixote's name, means "idealistic and impractical." The expression "tilting at windmills" also comes from this story.

ABOVE: *Plácido Domingo.*

ABOVE: *Montserrat Caballé.*

Food

Spaniards usually start the day with a very light breakfast (*desayuno*), often little more than coffee; they have brunch (*almuerzo*) around 10:30 a.m.; lunch (*comida*) between 1:30 and 4:00 p.m.; and dinner (*cena*) is as late as 10:00 or 11.00 p.m. Cafés are the centers of social activity in most cities and villages.

Tapas are also an important part of the Spaniards' way of life. These are little snacks that include things such as *calamares* (squid), *callos* (tripe), *gambas* (prawns), *albóndigas* (meatballs), and *boquerones* (anchovies) marinated in vinegar. Tapas can be taken as a meal in themselves or as a tasty bite before dinner. Each region of Spain has its own *tapa* specialties. Tapas bars have become popular eating places in the United States.

For centuries, Spain has been one of the world's great culinary centers. Its ancient roots in Africa and Rome, as well as Europe, have given it a unique flavor all its own. Because of its many colonies in the Americas, Spain's influence still reaches around the globe today.

ABOVE: *A* tapa *is a small dish of food, usually served in Spanish bars with drinks.*

Spanish Omelet
(Tortilla española)

Makes 3 servings

Ingredients
2 pounds potatoes
1 cup plus 1 tablespoon olive oil
4 eggs
dash of salt

Directions
Wash and cut the potatoes into thin slices. Heat 1 cup of the oil in the pan on medium high, and add the potatoes and salt. Fry, stirring occasionally. When the potatoes look golden brown, remove them from the pan and drain them on a paper towel. When well drained, place in a medium-sized bowl.

In a small bowl, beat the eggs well with a pinch of salt, and add to the potatoes. Mix well.

Reheat the oil, and once the oil is hot, add the potato and egg mixture. Shake the pan gently to move the mixture, so that none sticks to the bottom. Once the eggs seem solid, use the lid of the frying pan (or a large plate) to tip the omelet out of the pan. Add a little more oil and slide the omelet in again, this time putting the less cooked side first in to the pan. Cook until the omelet is golden on both sides.

Polvorones (Christmas cookies)

Makes 6 dozen

Ingredients
5 cups all-purpose flour
1¼ cups white sugar
2¾ cups melted shortening
¼ teaspoon ground cinnamon
½ ounce anise extract

Directions
Preheat the oven to 250° F. Combine the flour and cinnamon. Add the melted shortening and mix well. Stir in the anise and knead for 5 minutes. Roll into 1-inch balls and place 2 inches apart on an ungreased cookie sheet. Bake for 30 minutes. Cookies should remain pale. Dust with white sugar and allow to cool.

What Does *Tapa* Mean?

The actual translation of *tapa* is "lid." The story goes that bar owners used to cover drinks with a piece of bread to keep the flies away. It then became practice to put a tidbit of meat on the bread—and this evolved into the tapas of today.

ABOVE: *Dating from 1847, the April Fair (Feria de Abril) is a traditional festival that takes place in Seville. It takes place annually in April and lasts for a week.*

Spanish Pastimes

People in Spain love to go to the movies. They also enjoy plays, and most cities have theaters. Many of these were built by the socialist government in the 1980s and 90s.

One of the most important sports in Spain is football—or soccer, as it's called in North America. Around 300,000 spectators attend the games in the Primera División, and millions more follow the games on television. People gamble on

ABOVE: *Camp Nou, the famous stadium belonging to Barcelona football club.*

ABOVE: Dating from 1217, the famous La Boqueria market in Barcelona is one of the oldest markets in Europe. It is one of the city's foremost tourist destinations. It is close to many other shopping areas and is not far from the Liceu, Barcelona's opera house.

the football results through the *quiniela* or football pools.

La corrida de toros—the bullfight—may be considered cruel in North American culture, but it still has a following in Spain. It gained enormous popularity in the mid-eighteenth century, when breeders developed the first breeds of *toro bravo* or fighting bulls, and it still plays a role in Spanish culture. Today, fewer and fewer Spaniards support the pastime, and recent polls show that almost sixty percent of the population oppose it.

ABOVE: *The bullfighting arena in Seville.*

Text-Dependent Questions

1. What population groups are there in Spain?

2. What is the main religion in Spain?

3. What pastimes do Spanish people enjoy?

Research Project

Write a cultural history of a Spanish city or town, including famous painters who lived or worked there, important architecture, and the city's festivals.

Words to Understand

era: An important period of history.

fort: A strong or fortified place.

realms: Countries that are ruled by a king or queen.

BELOW: The Madrid skyline. Catedral de Santa María la Real de la Almudena is in the background and the Royal Palace of Madrid is in the foreground.

Chapter Five
THE FAMOUS CITIES OF SPAIN

Madrid

In the center of the Iberian Peninsula lies Madrid, the capital of Spain. Situated high on the Meseta (central plateau), Madrid is Europe's highest city (2,100 feet or 650 meters above sea level). A densely populated city, it is also home to art galleries and other cultural centers.

Although Madrid was once thought to have been founded by the Romans, historians now believe it was originally an Islamic **fort**, established in 854 CE. Madrid's Muslim **era** ended in 1085, when the region was handed to King Alfonso VI of Castile. Although its population is thought to have numbered around 12,000 at this time, the town was not considered to be a very important one.

While Madrid remained on the fringe of Spanish history, Isabella and Ferdinand united the Castilian and Aragonese **realms** in 1474, creating the original nation of Spain. Isabella and Ferdinand's grandson, Carlos I, succeeded not only to the throne of Spain but also to that of the Habsburgs, becoming

ABOVE: *The gardens at the Royal Palace of Madrid.*

Educational Video

A travel guide to Madrid.

ABOVE: *El Rastro de Madrid is a popular open-air flea market in Madrid selling new and used products. It is held every Sunday and on public holidays during the year. It is located along Plaza de Cascorro and Ribera de Curtidores.*

ABOVE: *Plaza de la Villa is one of Madrid's oldest squares. Renowned for its architecture, it is home to a number of historic buildings that today attract large numbers of visitors.*

Holy Roman Emperor over territories stretching from Austria to Holland and from Spain to the American colonies. But it was Carlos's son and successor, Felipe II, who made Madrid the permanent seat of the royal court in 1561.

Over the next century, as Spain's treasury was bled dry, the country's rulers retreated to Madrid, building a sumptuous fairy-tale land of palaces and elaborate cathedrals. Meanwhile, the ordinary people who lived in Madrid sank into abject poverty. Eventually, in the nineteenth century, the people of Madrid rose up and fought for independence. Their struggle only left the city exhausted and facing starvation.

Society in Madrid remained dominated by rich landowners, with the poorer classes still living in the city's slums. A full one-quarter of the working population was employed as servants in wealthy households. In 1837, the government took control of Church property, which helped build new middle class as working people could now afford to buy land. (Unfortunately, many great art treasures were destroyed in the process.) As more money came into the city, living conditions improved; street paving, gas lighting, sewage service, and garbage collection greatly improved Madrid's appearance.

Today, a revival of artistic and cultural activity is taking place in the city. The old city center is being restored, and public transport and public housing are also being improved. Madrid has the combined advantages of modern infrastructure and preserved heritage. Madrid is the most visited city of Spain.

ABOVE: *The Plaza de Cibeles is famous for the Palacio de Cibeles (City Hall), and the fountain of the same name.*

ABOVE: *The Cuatro Torres Business Area is the site of Madrid's tallest buildings.*

ABOVE: *Park Güell in Barcelona was designed by the renowned architect Antoni Gaudí. The park was built between 1900 and 1914 and opened in 1926. In 1984, the park was declared a World Heritage Site.*

Barcelona

On the shores of the Mediterranean Sea on the Iberian Peninsula's northeastern coast, Barcelona is the second-largest city in Spain in both size and population. It is also the capital of Catalonia, one of Spain's seventeen regional governments.

The city has a population of 1,600,000—or around four million if the outlying areas are also included. Barcelona's inhabitants speak two official languages: Catalan and Castilian Spanish.

Barcelona has a Mediterranean atmosphere, not only because of its geographic location but also because of its history, tradition, and cultural influences. The city dates back to the founding of a Roman colony in the

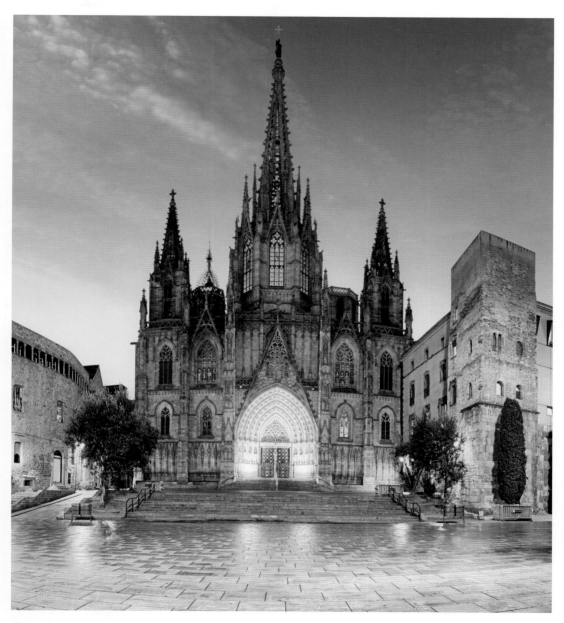

ABOVE: *Barcelona Cathedral (the Cathedral of the Holy Cross and Saint Eulalia) is situated in the Gothic Quarter. In addition to the cathedral, the area consists of narrow medieval streets filled with fashionable bars, clubs, cafés, and restaurants.*

second century BCE. At the beginning of the nineteenth century, with the arrival of modern industries, Barcelona experienced spectacular growth and economic revival. The 1888 World's Fair was held there and became a symbol of the city's international perspective, as well as its people's capacity for hard work. Culture and the arts flourished in Barcelona.

Today, Barcelona has many faces. It is an active, modern city—with a historic Gothic center. The Eixample, a carefully planned "Enlargement" project, is an

ABOVE: La Rambla in Barcelona is a famous part-pedestrianized street that is popular with tourists. It was the location of a terrorist attack in 2017.

ABOVE: *The well-known tourist attraction of Plaça Reial (Royal Plaza) is one of the most lively squares in Barcelona. It is located in the Gothic Quarter, close to La Rambla.*

area of grid-like streets, while other areas of the city are a maze of narrow, medieval lanes. These contrasts add to Barcelona's charm, making it particularly attractive to tourists.

Catalonia's parliament, based in Barcelona, has made a case for separating from the rest of Spain. In 2017, an independence referendum was held. However, Spanish police disrupted the referendum, causing injury to hundreds of people. Despite this, Catalonia declared independence. Following the disturbances, Spain imposed direct rule.

Seville

Seville, located in the southwest of Spain, is a provincial capital and the seat of the regional government, including its parliament. It has more than 700,000 inhabitants, which is nearly half the population of the entire region. The city of Seville is located on the plain of the Guadalquivir River. This river can be navigated from Seville all the way to its outlet on the Atlantic coast, which makes Seville a busy port. In 1492, the city played an important role in the discovery and conquest of America, serving as a vital link between Spain and the Americas; today, it remains one of the most active river ports of the Iberian Peninsula.

Centuries of Moorish rule in Seville (from 712 to 1248) left a permanent imprint on the city. La Giralda, the minaret of an important mosque, is the most well-known of the remaining Islamic monuments. The seventeenth century was

ABOVE: *The Plaza de España (Spanish Square) is located in the María Luisa Park. It was one of the main constructions of the Ibero-American Exposition World's Fair that took place in Seville in 1929.*

ABOVE: *The Torre del Oro (Tower of Gold) is a dodecagonal military watchtower in Seville. It was erected in the thirteenth century by the Almohad Caliphate in order to control access to Seville via the Guadalquivir River.*

a period of artistic creativity in Seville. Painters such as Veláquez, Murillo, and Valdés Leal, and sculptors like Martínez Montañés lived and worked here. The city also had an important role in world literature and was the birthplace of the myth of Don Juan, the famous lover.

Twice in the twentieth century, Seville has been in the spotlight of the world's attention. In 1929, it hosted the Latin American Exhibition, which left behind important improvements in the city. Years later, in 1992, Seville hosted another big event, the Expo 92 that showed it off as a modern, dynamic city.

The city is also credited with the invention of tapas. More than a thousand bars in Seville offer these tasty hors d'oeuvres, and the choice is virtually unlimited—from seafood to ham and sausage, and from vegetable to cheese. Many Sevillians make a meal of them, moving from bar to bar and trying one dish at a time.

Granada

Granada, the capital of the region with the same name, is in the eastern part of the Spanish area known as Andalusia. The city was built at the foot of the Sierra Nevada Mountains, where the Darro and Genil rivers flow together.

The Moors crossed the strait of Gibraltar in 711 and settled in what was then a small Visigoth town perched on a hill. When Muhammed I founded the Nasrid dynasty in 1232, the kingdom of Granada stretched from Gibraltar to Murcia. On a hill overlooking Granada, Muhammed I built the Alhambra, a sprawling palace-citadel comprised of royal residental quarters, court complexes flanked by official chambers, a bath, and a mosque.

ABOVE: *A view from the Mirador de la Lona Hotel in the old town of Granada. The Triumphal Square and the city's gate, Puerta de Elvira, can be seen from here.*

ABOVE: *The Alhambra is a palace and fortress complex whose oldest parts date from the ninth century. It is located on top of al-Sabika Hill, to the east of the city of Granada.*

ABOVE: *The Albaicín is a district of Granada. It retains the narrow winding streets of its medieval Moorish past that date back to even before the rise of the Nasrid Kingdom.*

The kingdom's splendor endured until the Moors were forced to surrender Granada to the Catholic Monarchs, King Ferdinand and Queen Isabella, in 1492. During the four and a half centuries of Muslim rule, however, a rich Islamic culture had flourished in Granada, leaving the city with amazing examples of Moorish architecture. The most famous of them, the Alhambra, has been declared a World Heritage Site.

As the last Moorish capital on the Iberian Peninsula, Granada has a rich heritage. Its unique history has bestowed it with an artistic wealth that includes Moorish palaces and Christian Renaissance treasures. The city brims with picturesque sites: steep, narrow streets, beautiful nooks and crannies, and marvelous landscapes.

Text-Dependent Questions

1. Which city is the capital of Spain?

2. Which city is the capital of Catalonia?

3. Where is the Alhambra and how old is it?

Research Project

Write an essay on tourism to Spanish cities. Explain which Spanish cities are the most attractive to tourists and why.

Words to Understand

austere: Without luxury, excess, or ease.

deficit: A shortage, especially in money.

strikers: Workers who stop work in order to force an employer to agree to their demands.

BELOW: Skyscrapers in Madrid's business district. The four towers, photographed here, are currently the highest buildings in Spain and some of the tallest in the European Union.

Chapter Six
A BRIGHT FUTURE FOR SPAIN

The Economy

The most immediate problem facing Spain as a nation is its economic issues. Spain had a tough time recovering from the global financial crisis of 2008. Since then, to aid economic recovery, Spain's government put into effect billions of euros of spending cuts, which helped to reduce the country's **deficit**.

The Spanish people had to endure a very **austere** budget. In response, the Spanish people took industrial action and **strikers** took to the streets of several Spanish cities across the country. The government passed labor laws that gave more rights to employers while taking them away from workers. Spain's people were worried.

Today, Spain's ongoing economic recovery remains highly vulnerable to the challenges related to the financial sector's competitiveness. Despite relatively sound economic institutions and good regulatory and legal systems, the indebted public sector is still a hindrance to the economy. A lack of progress has resulted in a high level of public debt that is close to the size of the economy.

ABOVE: *EU and Spanish flags.*

Climate Change

One of the big problems that threatens the future of the entire planet is global climate change. Spain has many strengths and it is working hard to overcome its problems—but the future for us all depends on the Earth's well-being. We can't fix the economy or society if we don't have a place to live!

ABOVE: *Photovoltaic panels for renewable energy production in Navarre.*

What Is Global Climate Change—and Why Are People So Worried About It?

Global climate change has to do with an average increase in the Earth's temperature. Most scientists agree that humans are responsible because of the pollution that cars and factories have put into the air.

Global warming is already having serious impacts on humans and the environment in many ways. An increase in global temperatures causes rising sea levels (because of melting of the polar caps) and changes in the amount and pattern of precipitation. These changes may increase the frequency and intensity of extreme weather events, such as floods, droughts, heat waves, hurricanes, and tornados. Other consequences include changes to farms' crop production, species becoming extinct, and an increased spread of disease.

Not all experts agree about climate change, but almost all scientists believe that it is very real. Politicians and the public do not agree, though, on policies to deal with climate change. Changes in the way people live can be expensive, at both the personal and national levels, and not everyone is convinced that taking on these expenses needs to be a priority.

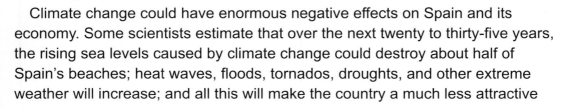

Climate change could have enormous negative effects on Spain and its economy. Some scientists estimate that over the next twenty to thirty-five years, the rising sea levels caused by climate change could destroy about half of Spain's beaches; heat waves, floods, tornados, droughts, and other extreme weather will increase; and all this will make the country a much less attractive

ABOVE: *Wooden sherry barrels at the world-famous Gonzalez Byass cellar at Jerez de la Frontera, Andalusia.*

spot for tourists. Without its tourist industry, Spain's economy will be in trouble. Farming will also suffer as a result of climate change.

Spain's government recognizes that climate change will cause water shortages. With help from the EU, the country is building desalination plants to try to deal with this problem. Not all experts agree, however, that this is a good idea. Ecologists warn that desalination uses up a lot of energy, and it also puts carbon dioxide into the atmosphere (which will further contribute to global warming). Many experts recommend that Spain instead build the technology for capturing and storing its rainwater.

The EU has sustainable energy goals for all its member nations. Spain will have a hard time complying with these goals. Farmers and industries tend to want short-term solutions rather than paying the price for long-term answers.

But Spain remains committed to the European Union. It knows that by saying yes to the EU, Spain is also saying yes to the future.

Food and Drinks Industry

The Spanish food and drinks industry is a great success story. It had its best ever year in 2016–17, breaking production, export, and employment records.

Figures released by the Spanish Federation of Food and Beverage Industries reveal that the growing popularity of Spanish produce is growing year-on-year. The food and drinks industry now represents 11 percent of the country's total goods exports.

Spain is the sixth-highest food and drinks exporter in the EU and the tenth highest globally. It is predicted that if this upward trend continues, the country will overtake competitors such as Belgium or Italy in the near future. Meat products are Spain's largest exports, followed by olive oil, fish products, and wine.

The majority of products are exported to the EU, but fortunately for the Spanish economy, exports are growing steadily to the USA, China, and Japan. Furthermore, the number of people employed in the country's food and drinks sector has gone up for the last three years.

The range of produce made for export originates in regions from all over Spain. Products include Spanish wines, Iberian hams, and the purest oils, Manchego cheese, sausages, and pickles. Spanish foods are becoming increasingly in fashion and sought-after.

In addition to luxury foods, Spain is a major supplier of fruit and vegetables to the EU and also to the rest of the world.

ABOVE: *Spanish chorizo sausage is exported all over the world.*

ABOVE: *New cars at Barcelona port waiting to be exported.*

Automotive Industry

Compared with other European countries, Spain was relatively slow to develop its car industry. However, during the 1960s, government policy helped transform car production in Spain. By the the 1980s, the Spanish automotive company, SEAT, was sold to the Volkswagen group, which gave a tremendous boost to profitability and helped to create a manufacturing cluster attracting other international manufacturers to Spain.

Today, Spain is in the top ten of automobile producers in the world, producing a total of 2.8 million vehicles in 2016, from which about 80 percent is for export. During the first half of 2016, car exports were valued at over €24 billion over that period. The automotive industry as a whole accounted for 18.9 percent of total Spanish exports.

In all, there are thirteen car factories located in Spain, which are supported by a thriving local car components industry, including rapidly growing Spanish multinationals such as Gestamp Automoción or Grupo Antolin. The main manufacturers established in the country are Daimler AG (manufacturing plant in Vitoria), Ford (its plant located in Almussafes is Ford's biggest in Europe), General Motors (Figueruelas), Nissan (Barcelona), PSA Peugeot Citroen (Vigo), Renault (with plants in Palencia and other Spanish locations), SEAT (Martorell), and Volkswagen (Pamplona). From these production plants, as of 2016, the two biggest by volume are the ones of SEAT in Martorell and PSA in Vigo.

Text-Dependent Questions

1. Why is the Spanish government concerned about climate change?

2. What is Spain's largest food export?

3. Who bought SEAT, the Spanish car producer?

Research Project

Write an essay on the history of Spanish sherry, explaining where it is produced, how it is made, and how important it is to the Spanish economy.

CHRONOLOGY

8000–4000 BCE	50,000–30,000 BCE Earliest modern humans move into the Iberian Peninsula.
800	Celts arrive at the northern part of the Iberian Peninsula.
206	Roman Empire invades Spain.
4th century CE	Spain becomes Christian.
711	Moors invade the Iberian Peninsula.
854	Madrid is established.
1474	Marriage of Queen Isabella and King Ferdinand unite Castilian and Aragonese realms to create the nation of Spain.
1492	Queen Isabella and King Ferdinand finance Christopher Columbus's trip to the New World.
1561	Madrid becomes permanent seat of the royal court.
1713	Spain cedes Gibraltar to Great Britain.
1929	Seville hosts the Latin American Exhibition.
1931	King Alfonso XIII abdicates the Spanish throne and Spain is declared a republic.
1942	Ferdinand Franco assumes complete control of Spain.
1951	The Treaty of Paris is signed, forming the core of what would become the EU.
1959	Basque homeland and liberty (ETA) forms.
1978	Spain's constitution creates the Cortes, Spain's parliament.
1986	Spain joins the European Community.
1992	The European Union is formed under the Maastricht Treaty.
2004	A terrorist bomb on the Madrid train system kills almost two hundred people.
2008	Global recession spreads around the world.
2011	The ETA commits to a permanent ceasefire.
2014	King Juan Carlos abdicates and is succeeded Felipe VI.
2017	Two terror attacks involving people driving vehicles at crowds at high speed, the one on Las Ramblas boulevard in Barcelona killing 13 and injuring more than 100 people.
2017	Catalonia holds an independence referendum, which is deemed unlawful by the Spanish government.

Further Reading

Ardagh, John. Baird, David. Gallagher, Mary-Ann. Hayward, Vicky. Hopkins, Adam. Hunt, Lindsay. Inman, Nick. Richardson, Paul. Symington, Martin. Tisdall, Nigel. Williams, Roger. *DK Eyewitness Travel Guide: Spain*. London: DK, 2016.

McCormick, John. *Understanding the European Union: A Concise Introduction. London:* Palgrave Macmillan, 2017.

Mason, David S. *A Concise History of Modern Europe: Liberty, Equality, Solidarity.* London: Rowman & Littlefield, 2015.

Steves, Rick. *Rick Steves Spain*. Edmonds: Rick Steves' Europe, Inc., 2018.

Internet Resources

Spain Travel Information and Travel Guide
https://www.lonelyplanet.com/spain

Spain Tourism Official
http://www.spain.info

Spain: Country Profile
http://www.bbc.co.uk/news/world-europe-17941641

Spain: CIA World Factbook
https://www.cia.gov/library/publications/the-world-factbook/geos/sp.html

The Official Website of the European Union
europa.eu/index_en.htm

Publisher's note:
The websites listed on this page were active at the time of publication. The publisher is not responsible for websites that have changed their addresses or discontinued operation since the date of publication. The publisher will review and update the website list upon each reprint.

Picture Credits

All images in this book are in the public domain or have been supplied under license by © Shutterstock.com. The publisher credits the following images as follows:

Page 37, 38, 59: 360b, page 42: Roman Yanushevsky, page 42: Daniel Leppens, page 46: Concealed Resonancies, page 47: Nejron Photo, page 59 bottom: ToskkanalNC, page 62: Javaman, page 63 Natursports, page 65: Capture Light, page 68: pedro Rufo, page 71: David Herraez Calzada, page 74: Philip Lange, page 75: Mihai-Bogdan Lazar, Page 83: ChrisPictures, page 86: Miquelito.
Wikimedia Commons and the following:
page 32: IngenieroLoco, page 34: Estena.
To the best knowledge of the publisher, all images not specifically credited are in the public domain. If any image has been inadvertently uncredited, please notify the publisher, so that credit can be given in future printings.

Video Credits

Page 12 STRATFORvideo: http://x-qr.net/1DwL
page 26 PimsleurApproach: http://x-qr.net/1Hai
page 46 The Economist: http://x-qr.net/1FWL
page 68 Lonely Planet: http://x-qr.net/1HSG

Author

Dominic J. Ainsley is a freelance writer on history, geography, and the arts and the author of many books on travel. His passion for traveling dates from when he visited Europe at the age of ten with his parents. Today, Dominic travels the world for work and pleasure, documenting his experiences and encounters as he goes. He lives in the south of England in the United Kingdom with his wife and two children.